Journey with Jesus

" 'Come, follow me,' Jesus said. . . ."

Matthew 4:19, NIV

Journey *with* JESUS

K.P. Yohannan

a division of Gospel for Asia
www.gfa.org

Journey with Jesus

ISBN: 978-1-59589-018-4

Published by gfa books, a division of Gospel for Asia
1800 Golden Trail Court, Carrollton, TX 75010 USA
phone: (972) 300-7777
fax: (972) 300-7778

Printed in the United States of America

For information about other materials, visit our website: www.gfa.org.

09 10 11 12 / 6 5 4

Table of Contents

Introduction

Through the years I have been in ministry, I have found that the best way to encourage others in living a life of Christlike character is not in a classroom full of methods and rules, but rather as Jesus taught—through everyday life events.

Through the pages of this booklet, it is my desire to walk together with you and point out the ways Jesus responded to the situations and the people He met while on this earth. From His love and humility to His power and obedience, I pray that the message of this booklet would encourage you to continue your journey with Jesus, no matter what comes your way. For it is as we see Jesus in every moment of our lives that we not only learn from Him, but come to mirror Him as well, reflecting His character to everyone around us. In doing so, we bring glory to our God and Father. This is the desire of my heart, and I believe it is the desire of your heart as well.

CHAPTER ONE

Lord, Teach Us

In this day and age, when a person desires to learn something new or become skilled in a particular field, he will seek some form of educational institution, be it a college or technical school, master's program or certification. Years are spent, reports are written and book after book is studied, all to gain the desired knowledge.

But in ancient times, a different form of learning took place. Students lived with their teachers, learning directly from watching their lives, pulling valuable lessons and asking necessary questions from daily events. The home was the classroom; the textbook was living examples and events of the day.

Look through the Gospels and you will see that this is the way Jesus taught His disciples. Through everyday events, Jesus revealed what the Father God was like. Whatever came His way became His teaching material—a child's illness, a crowd of hungry people, the woman caught in adultery, the disciples' dusty feet or a confrontation by the high priest's troops.

Jesus' reason for taking 12 men to be His disciples was to teach them—through His example and the events of life—how to live like Him and do what He did. And the Bible shows how effective He was in that. Consider the time when the disciples asked Jesus to teach them: "One day Jesus was praying in a certain place. When he finished, one of his disciples said to him, 'Lord, teach us to pray . . .' " (Luke 11:1, NIV). And Jesus taught them!

But the teaching was not an end in itself. It was not knowledge for knowledge's sake, but rather to spur them into action. And that's just what happened—"Calling the Twelve to him, he sent them out two by two and gave them authority over evil spirits . . . . They went out and preached that people should repent. They drove out many demons and anointed many sick people with oil and healed them" (Mark 6:7, 12–13, NIV).

Up until this point, all the disciples had

known were fishing nets and village life. Yet now they were doing the very works of Jesus! Later, in the book of Acts, we see how these ordinary men went on to evangelize their entire world, suffering great persecution yet enduring until the end. Think of where they began. How were they able to do what they did and make such an incredible impact on their world? I believe it is only because they saw Jesus. They walked with Him. They watched His life. They saw His passion. They saw His humility and His great love portrayed in so many ways, time and time again. And they were changed by what they saw. Changed forever.

Jesus desires the same for us today. We are given the accounts of Jesus' life not just for the sake of knowing how He lived, but so that we, in seeing Him, might be changed—changed into the very image of Christ. Then we, like the disciples, can go and live for Him, suffer for Him and make a lasting difference on our world.

If your heart is open and you desire to journey with Him, He will teach you who He is and His ways through the very events of your own life. Receive His invitation today.

CHAPTER TWO

How Lives Are Built

A good portion of my time is often spent with younger leaders who are experiencing some sort of difficult situation in their life or ministry. I try to help these brothers grow through the adverse circumstances of life to become more effective in their work for the Lord and to become even better leaders. The only way I can do this, though, is by showing them Jesus.

For example, several months ago one of our leaders called to tell me about a problem with which he was dealing. This particular leader had spent several years training two brothers, discipling and entrusting them with a great amount of responsibility in the work. One day, unexpectedly, they walked away from the work and joined another organization.

Not only was he upset over the situation, but also very discouraged, having lost two people he deeply cared about. As I spoke with him over the phone he said, "I wish they at least would have told me a few weeks earlier, so that I could have made arrangements for others to take over their responsibilities." He continued to express his disappointment with a saddened heart. I asked him if he knew the reason why these brothers left. He said, "The truth of the matter is the other organization offered them a lot of money and material benefits, and that became the reason for their leaving."

Of course, the whole reason this leader called me in the first place was to hear what I thought his next step should be. Instead of telling him "do this" or "do that," I asked him to think with me about how Jesus would respond had He been in this situation. Together we recalled certain passages of Scripture, remembering that it was Jesus who said, "Bless those who curse you, pray for those who mistreat you. If someone strikes you on one cheek, turn to him the other also. If someone takes your cloak, do not stop him from taking your tunic. Give to everyone who asks you, and if anyone takes what belongs to you, do not demand it back" (Luke 6:28–30, NIV).

It was soon clear how Jesus would respond. This leader decided to write a letter to the head of the organization the men had joined and say all the good things he could about the two brothers who had left him. He blessed that ministry and the two brothers, promising to pray for them as they continued to serve the Lord.

It is in responding like this, in a way that mirrors Christ, that lives are built.

We all desire to become mature Christians and to be used by God. And we all have difficulties in our life as well. What we must see is that maturity often comes only through difficulty—it does not occur in a vacuum or a totally sterile and completely peaceful and happy environment in which we always get what we want. No. Christian maturity—Christlikeness—happens only as we live like Him in this fallen world. Through difficulties, God works maturity into our lives, producing good in us, to the praise of the Father!

As Jesus' ministry on this earth was soon coming to an end, He prayed for the disciples and for all those who would come to believe on His name some day. It is interesting what He prayed: "I do not pray that You should take them out of the world, but that You should keep them from the evil one" (John 17:15). Jesus left us in the world, not to become a part of it but to learn more of Him through each trial and tribulation. As we see Jesus in the midst of our days, just as the disciples did, our lives are shaped and we are made into His image.

We are in the world to be changed into His likeness and to reflect His character and glory in every situation. Hebrews 5:8 says that Jesus "learned obedience by the things which He suffered." If the Son of God learned obedience through the things He experienced on the earth, then the same should be true for us.

Think about Abraham, Moses, Daniel, Gideon, Peter or Paul. Read about the lives of modern-day saints like Sadhu Sundar Singh, Pandita Ramabai, John Hyde, George Muller or Gladys Aylward. These people were made and shaped into those whom we esteem today by the difficulties and hardships they endured. They allowed themselves to be taught by God in each situation.

We must keep in mind, though, that this is a continual, daily process; none of us is fashioned into the image of Christ overnight.

It takes years and many situations, but as you continue to choose to reflect Jesus in every situation, He will transform you to live this life pleasing to Him, bringing Him glory. And in each event we face, we can have the confident hope that "all things work together for good to those who love God, to those who are the called according to His purpose. For whom He foreknew, He also predestined to be conformed to the image of His Son" (Romans 8:28–29).

It is His grace that allows us to respond in this life as He would. It is His strength that carries us along this journey to learn from Him and become like Him. Jesus still calls to us today saying, "Come to Me . . . and *learn from Me* . . . " (Matthew 11:28–29, emphasis mine). Please, I urge you, open your Bible and step into your own journey with Jesus. Ask the Holy Spirit to help you see Jesus through the pages of Scripture and to show you how to imitate Him in your life situations today. Just like the disciples, it is only as we see Jesus that we become like Him and make a difference in our generation.

CHAPTER THREE

A New Commandment

In John 13:34–35 (NIV), Jesus said to His disciples, "A new command I give you: Love one another. As I have loved you, so you must love one another. By this all men will know that you are my disciples, if you love one another."

We've all had times in our lives when we have been hurt, perhaps by someone we know very well or someone we know just casually, and we find loving that person to be very difficult. Hurtful and trying experiences that cause much pain are part of life—even Jesus experienced them. What is important is how we respond in those times, for that determines the growth that will or will not occur in our lives. In seeing Jesus' response, we can gain the strength and grace to do the same and come one step closer to mirroring Him.

Steadfast Love

Imagine the topic of conversation among the disciples after the crucifixion and resurrection of Christ. I'm sure their minds strained to remember each event and how it related to what came to pass, recalling their times with the Lord, the days leading up to the crucifixion and the dramatic and prophetic unfolding of every moment.

Perhaps they recalled their own Judas, remembering how he left right in the middle of the Last Supper. By this time, the disciples knew that Judas was the one who had betrayed the Lord and that he had hung himself from the guilt of it. I can just hear one of the disciples saying, "I can't believe Jesus didn't just throw Judas out from the start! He had to have known all along that he was stealing money. And certainly He knew that Judas was the one who would betray Him in the end. Why did He let him stick around? At least Jesus could have told us that he was the one who was going to betray Him, so that we would have known to stay away from him."

And then I can hear someone like Peter speaking up, saying, "Well, I'm not surprised at the way Jesus treated Judas. Jesus loved us until the very end and that includes him. I betrayed Jesus as well; I denied Him—and not just once, but *three* times. With His own eyes He saw me turn my back on Him. Yet when He rose again, He specifically called out my name and said, 'Go and tell Peter.' When He found me I was ashamed, discouraged and backslidden. But when I first saw Him after the resurrection, all I saw were His love and His mercy. Not once did He bring up my turning away or reprimand me and tell me how wrong I was. He simply came close and asked, 'Do you love Me?'

"No, I'm not surprised He loved Judas. He loved each one of us. And we must never forget what He told us: that we must love one another as He loved us."

The disciples' lives were completely transformed by what they saw in Jesus. They watched Him respond to beggars, hold little children and heal the blind. But what impacted them even more was what they saw in Him *after* the resurrection—the forgiveness and love *after* the betrayal and turning away, the joy with which He showed them the scars in His hands and side (see Luke 24:39) and the camaraderie displayed as He cooked breakfast for them on the beach after a long night of toil (see John 21:9).

I believe that the only reason the disciples were able to impact their world in such a great way and endure such intense persecution was because of the unfailing love they saw in Jesus. It was this love that enabled Stephen to suffer and die for the Lord in Acts 7, crying out for his persecutors just as Jesus did, saying, "Lord, do not charge them with this sin" (Acts 7:60). "Love covers a multitude of sins" (1 Peter 4:8, NIV).

Only as we behold Christ, aware of His presence and remembering the ultimate love He *always* displayed, can we begin to reflect His love to those around us.

Love Is Costly

The story is told that when the apostle John was a very old man who could hardly walk, the believers would carry him and sit him before the congregation to share. It is said that the only thing he could say was repeatedly the phrase, "Love one another. Love one another."

In John 13, Jesus spoke directly to His disciples about loving one another: "A new commandment I give to you, that you love one another; as I have loved you, that you also love one another" (John 13:34). Up until this point, the disciples had only seen how Christ loved them and those around them. This is the first time that He calls them to love one another just as they had seen Him love them. Jesus was essentially saying to them, "I'm just about to leave now. But I want you to understand this one thing—love each other. Love has been the foundation of everything I have done. So too it must be with each of you."

Love was the bedrock of Jesus' life, the very reason He came to seek and save the lost. "For God so loved the world that He gave His only begotten Son" (John 3:16). Therefore, love must be the bedrock of our lives. No matter what good we do in life, it all must flow from the spring of Christ's love within our hearts.

Yet even in the familiarity of Bible verses, we still find it difficult to love one another. Why is that? One of the reasons is because we do not want to pay the price. You see, love is always costly.

John 3:16 says, "For God so *loved* the world that He *gave* . . . " (emphasis mine). Gave what? What was the price of God's love? His Son, Jesus. The cross was the price

God paid because of His love for us.

We can ask ourselves the same question: What is the price of our love? Put your name in that verse, "For __________ so loved that he/she gave . . . " Gave what? The price of love will differ in form for each one of us, but God will always bring us opportunities to display His love to others. But remember, the price will always be costly—it will always involve saying "no" to self in some way. It could be quietly suffering and not defending yourself. It could be going the extra mile and taking the slack when somebody else didn't do the job. But whatever it is, God has brought these situations into your life to make you more like His Son, enabling you to display His love through your life.

One of our missionaries in India showed incredible love for a man in a remarkable way. While working in a particular village for a couple of years, this missionary was continually opposed by one certain man. The man would adamantly hinder the missionary as he preached the Gospel and won people to Christ, even gathering groups of people to destroy the Christian literature and beat up the believers in the village.

One day, the man who opposed our missionary and the local church had a horrible accident in which both of his legs were broken. Deserted by all his friends, he lay in his hut, penniless and without help.

When our missionary found out about this man's accident, he didn't let out a sigh of relief, glad that this man could no longer oppose him in his work of the Gospel. Instead, our missionary decided to seize this opportunity to show the love of Christ to the very one who opposed him. He called together the believers in the village, and each donated a few rupees to pay for the man's hospital visit. Then our missionary visited him in his hut and carried him on his back for seven kilometers to the main road, where they caught a Jeep to the hospital.

After a month, the injured man fully recovered from his accident. The first thing he said when he saw the missionary was, "I cannot persist. I cannot oppose you any more. Jesus and His love, which I have seen and experienced through you and your church members, are so real. Thank you so much for loving me even when I hated you and hated Christ."

This, my friends, is the love of Christ in action. Remember, "God demonstrates His own love toward us, in that while we were still sinners, Christ died for us" (Romans 5:8).

Could you love like this? Could you love the one who has hurt you deeply? Could you love the one who is opposing you? When you feel that doing so is simply impossible, remember Christ. Look to Him and allow Him to take you by the hand and give you the grace to love like Him. We can love others only because He first loved us (see 1 John 4:19). Genuine love comes from Him; as we stand in His presence, it will flow from us as well.

CHAPTER FOUR

As I Have Done

In John 13, we see the beautiful place of humility the Son of God took before His own disciples. The passage reads,

> It was just before the Passover Feast. Jesus knew that the time had come for him to leave this world and go to the Father. Having loved his own who were in the world, he now showed them the full extent of his love.
>
> So he got up from the meal, took off his outer clothing, and wrapped a towel around his waist. After that, he poured water into a basin and began to wash his disciples' feet, drying them with the towel that was wrapped around him.

> When he had finished washing their feet, he put on his clothes and returned to his place. "Do you understand what I have done for you?" he asked them. "You call me 'Teacher' and 'Lord,' and rightly so, for that is what I am. Now that I, your Lord and Teacher, have washed your feet, you also should wash one another's feet. I have set you an example that you should do as I have done for you" (John 13:1, 4–5, 12–15, NIV).

In the Asian culture, it is difficult to even grasp this kind of event taking place! A master stooping down to wash his servants' feet?! Only slaves do that! Yet here we see the Creator of the universe, the Lord of lords and the King of kings who became the Son of Man, bending down to wash the dusty feet of His disciples.

Everywhere you travel across this world, you will find people driven to exalt themselves, some in a blatant manner and some in subtle ways, but all somehow driven to be recognized and known. But in John 13, we see the exact opposite happening. The One who, above all else, should be exalted, here is stooping low. And not low before powerful kings and rulers, but before ordinary men—His own disciples—men rough around the edges, feet worn and dusty from days of travel. All for one reason: "I have given you an example, that *you should do as I have done to you*" (John 13:15, emphasis mine).

In the early years of my serving the Lord, I struggled with this inner desire to be recognized and esteemed, as I'm sure many of us do, even in Christian service. However, this should really have no place in the life of the child of God.

When we behold Christ and realize the example He has given us, our lives and our pride should immediately bow—not just because of what was done, but because of *who* did it! If the Son of God could humble Himself before His disciples, how can I not humble myself in dealing with my brothers and sisters?

Every situation that comes in our lives in which we feel that inner urge to fight for our way needs to be seen as an instrument of God to shape us into a humble servant. As we choose to bow low, just like Jesus, we begin to mirror Him. And each day becomes more and more, "He must increase . . . I must decrease" (John 3:30).

Consider the position that 1 Peter 5:5–6 (NIV) tells us to take: "All of you, clothe yourselves with humility toward one another, because, 'God opposes the proud but gives grace to the humble.' Humble yourselves, therefore, under God's mighty hand, that he may lift you up in due time."

Oftentimes when we read this verse, we think the part that says, "He will lift you up" automatically means positions, titles, degrees or recognition. But this is far from what Christ meant. Humility cannot be used as a stepping stone to personal promotion. It is a dangerous thing for those in the Lord's service to live with the secret desire to be recognized, feel important, "climb the ladder" or be esteemed and rewarded by men.

Humility allows Christ's life to be perfected in us. But pride, the opposite of humility, works death in us. To be exalted, honored and recognized was the desire of Lucifer. He was not content with what God had chosen for him so he decided to exalt himself: "I will ascend into heaven, I will exalt my throne above the stars of God" (Isaiah 14: 13). Because of this Lucifer fell, rejected by God because of the pride in his heart. All sin originated in pride and self-exaltation. But our salvation originated in Christ *humbling* Himself by His death on the cross.

Philippians 2:3–4 tells us, "Let nothing be done through selfish ambition or conceit, but in lowliness of mind let each esteem others better than himself. Let each of you look out not only for his own interests, but also for the interests of others."

How does that translate into our lives? We can say with our lips, "I am small," but in our minds we are big. We have our education, our position and our possessions. We can look at someone and say, "This person is more important than I am" all we want. But we must live that out, demonstrating humility, if we are to be changed.

In dealing with others, it helps if we realize that we could be in another's situation. If it weren't for the grace of God, that beggar on the street could be me.

In the late 1960s when I was in Rajasthan, we would hire three-wheel rickshaw taxis to get us around. The passengers would sit on the back seat with their luggage, while the rickshaw driver would sit on the front seat and pedal. For two hours of pedaling, a driver would commonly receive about 10 rupees (equivalent to about 20 U.S. cents).

One day, I was riding in a rickshaw on my way to a meeting. It was the middle of summer, and the heat was overwhelming. As I sat in the back seat of the rickshaw, I watched my driver. He was an old man, all skin and bones, the veins in his neck bulging from the strain and the heat. He had no shirt on, and sweat poured down his body. "This is terrible!" I thought to myself. Here was this old man pedaling so hard to get me up this huge hill, in the middle of the summer heat. Certainly I had much more strength than he. I said to myself, "If it were not for the grace of God, I would be doing this job."

So I told the driver to stop the rickshaw. He quit pedaling and, concerned he had done something wrong, asked, "What happened?" I said, "Nothing is wrong. I just want you to give me the handlebars and you go and sit on the back." He couldn't believe it! I got on the front seat of that rickshaw and pedaled the rest of the way. When I got to my destination, I gave him a Gospel tract and paid him more money than he deserved. The man was blown away by what he had witnessed and experienced.

Truth is, I never could have done something like that if I thought I was better than that man. It is only in seeing Christ's humility and esteeming others better than myself that I am able to love my fellow man and walk humbly with him. As we embrace these opportunities, the sweet love of Jesus flows out of our lives, drawing all men to Him.

Again and again, as the disciples traveled with Jesus, they saw His humility, His tears and His gentleness. Anyone could approach Him; there was no high-mindedness in His response to anyone. From the worst in the society to the most refined in the community, all could approach Him. He who knew their every sin and flaw still embraced them. Each was treated with dignity and compassion. This is the humility of Christ. And He did this so that we might do as He has done.

CHAPTER FIVE

Nothing of My Own

How many times must the disciples have heard Jesus say, "I do nothing of my own. I do only what My Father tells Me" (paraphrase, see John 5:19, 8:28)?

One of the many examples of this is found in John 11. Lazarus, the man Jesus loved dearly, is terribly sick. So his sisters send word to Jesus to come quickly to their aid, I'm sure with the hope that perhaps Jesus will heal him.

Upon hearing of His friend's sickness, I am certain that many emotions were stirred in Jesus' heart. Just imagine how you would feel if your closest and dearest friend was terribly ill and dying in the hospital. Would you not rush to your friend's aid, laying aside your plans and agendas just to be with him in his time of need?

Jesus was fully God and fully man, so I am sure that He very much wanted to make the trip immediately, to go and touch His friend Lazarus and raise him up. When He heard about Lazarus's sickness, He was about 30 miles away from the town he lived in—at least a two-day journey! But the Bible does not tell us that Jesus rushed out the door to go to Lazarus. Instead, "When Jesus heard that, He said, 'This sickness is not unto death, but for the glory of God, that the Son of God may be glorified through it.' Now Jesus loved Martha and her sister and Lazarus. So, when He heard that he was sick, *He stayed two more days in the place where He was*" (John 11:4–6, emphasis mine).

Later in the chapter we read of Jesus finally arriving at the tomb of Lazarus, who had now already been dead for four days. Both Mary and Martha cried to Him, "Lord, if You had been here, [our] brother would not have died" (John 11:21).

Why was Jesus not there sooner? Why didn't He go right away, as soon as He heard the news, before Lazarus died?

The answer is found in John 5:19—"The

Son can do nothing of Himself." The moment Jesus heard the news about Lazarus, He looked up and asked His Father what He must do. The Father must have told Him, "Son, it is not the time. Wait." And so Christ waited, demonstrating absolute submission to His Father's will.

And again, in the last few minutes of Jesus' life, before going to the cross, the disciples witnessed Christ kneeling and again talking to His Father, saying, "Father, if it is Your will, take this cup away from Me; nevertheless *not My will, but Yours, be done*" (Luke 22:42, emphasis mine). It was the Father's will for the Son to drink the cup that He gave Him. Even though inside Jesus pleaded for it to be taken from Him, He yielded to the will of His Father. In life and in death, Christ showed how He submitted Himself to His Father's will and authority, leaving this as an example for His disciples—and us—to follow.

Jesus was not only referring to submitting to spiritual authority either. He submitted to the governing authorities of His day as well, subject to the decisions of Herod and Pontius Pilate. If Christ, the One who rules the nations and sits at the right-hand throne of God, came to this earth and submitted to the leaders of His day, how much more should we?

How does Jesus' example apply to our lives? Sometimes the leadership God places in our lives may be younger than we or perhaps less able or wise in our eyes. We must recognize that God is the One who placed those individuals over us. Romans 13:1–2 (NIV) says, "Everyone must submit himself to the governing authorities, for there is no authority except that which God has established. The authorities that exist have been established by God. Consequently, he who rebels against the authority is rebelling against what God has instituted, and those who do so will bring judgment on themselves." We cannot break God's order.

Jesus recognized in the garden of Gethsemane, as the Roman soldiers came to take Him away, that they "could have no power at all against [Him] unless it had been given [them] from above" (John 19:11). And we must recognize the same in our lives, allowing each circumstance to be used as the tool to produce in us the submission and humility of Christ.

In Judges 7, we find the story of Gideon and his army. Starting at 32,000 men, Gideon's army was quickly reduced to 10,000, and again until only 300 men, chosen by God, marched with him. That's less than one percent of what he started with! But Gideon didn't need a large army—only a small one that would *simply follow instructions.*

According to simple math and logic, the men in his army were incredibly outnumbered and doomed to die by the massive, opposing army. But according to the plan and instructions of the Lord, Gideon readied his men, giving each a clay pot containing a torch inside (see Judges 7:16). He then turned to his army and said, "Look at me and do likewise; watch, and when I come to the edge of the camp you shall do as I do" (Judges 7:17). Gideon had his men surround the enemy, holding these clay pots in their hands. When he gave them the go-ahead, the men were to break the pots and cause the light to shine out (see Judges 7). They followed Gideon's command and defeated their enemy that day.

These 300 men were totally committed to following Gideon's instruction regardless of how illogical it seemed. They had no opinion of their own or suggestions for Gideon on how to win the battle. Their attitude was, "Whatever you say, we will do." Their submission to the authority of their leader was complete. And so it must be in our lives—total submission to God our Father and the leaders He places over us.

In 2 Corinthians 4:7, Paul writes, "But we have this treasure in earthen vessels, that the excellence of the power may be of God and not of us." But unless we come to the place of giving up our stubborn will, our own ambitions and our way of doing things, the light of Christ will never shine out from us, the earthen vessels.

A.W. Tozer once said, "God cannot use a man greatly until He has broken him deeply." I believe this is true. If Jesus had not submitted and listened to the Father concerning Lazarus, the glory and power of God would not have been displayed through his resurrection. If Gideon's men decided their leader was foolish and therefore did not submit and follow his command, the battle never would have been won, nor the victory given to God. Jesus has set before us His submission as an example that we might do exactly as He has done.

First Corinthians 4:2 (TLB) says, "Now the most important thing about a servant is that he does just what his master tells him to." Let us then press on to follow our Master—Jesus—and live this kind of life pleasing to Him, sustained by the submission, humility and love that we see in Him.

CHAPTER SIX

In the Vine

After living a perfect, sinless life for 30 years, Jesus began His ministry, but not before He was anointed by the Holy Spirit. This same act was repeated before the disciples entered into their ministry after the resurrection of Christ. In Acts 1:4–8, we find Jesus speaking with His disciples, commanding them:

> . . . not to depart from Jerusalem, but to wait for the Promise of the Father, "which . . . you have heard from Me; for John truly baptized with water, but you shall be baptized with the Holy Spirit not many days from now. . . . [And] you shall receive power when the Holy Spirit

> has come upon you; and you shall be witnesses to Me in Jerusalem, and in all Judea and Samaria, and to the end of the earth."

Whatever theory or doctrine you hold on the Holy Spirit, there is one point on which we all can agree—that we *must* be filled with the Holy Spirit. Ephesians 5:18 exhorts us to not be filled with wine, which causes our ruin, but rather to "be filled with the Spirit." And we are encouraged to be *continually* filled, just as the disciples were in Acts 13:52 (NASB)—"And the disciples were continually filled with joy and with the Holy Spirit."

In the early days of my Christian work, I was very busy preaching and teaching in North India. Every night I was speaking somewhere, to some group of people. But inside I felt so dry and so empty. I desperately wished that somebody else would do the job.

But I'll never forget one day in Jammu when everything changed. An evening meeting was scheduled, and a very large crowd was expected to attend. A few hours before the event started I was in my room, kneeling beside my bed and crying out to God. My life had been a day-after-day struggle to spiritually stay alive as I served the Lord. And that night it was the same. I was so empty. I had my message. I had my outlines. I had my illustrations. I had everything together and ready to go, but still I was empty. I prayed like I had never prayed before, saying, "Lord, I don't know what to tell You. I am so dry, so empty. There is nothing in me. It's all in my head, but there is nothing in my heart. I have been going on week after week, pushing myself. Lord, I read in your Word about this thing called 'the power of the Holy Spirit.' I don't know what I must do, but I ask You, would You please fill me with Your Holy Spirit and give me the power to minister tonight in Your name?"

That night the most incredible thing happened. Between the time I prayed and when the meeting started, it was like I had grabbed hold of 100,000 watts of electricity. I was changed that night. Honestly, I don't even know all that happened, but I was never the same and the meeting was like no other. Hundreds of people wept and came forward to receive Christ. I didn't even preach from my outline because the Lord stepped in and my plans went out the window. That was one of the most significant moments in my entire life of serving the Lord.

So much of our daily life becomes a struggle because we live without the power of the Holy Spirit. Our lives often resemble the hand pumps along the roadsides in North India; if you want any water, you must continually crank the handle, sometimes just to get a single drop. As soon as you stop pumping the handle, everything stops. This is not the kind of life that was intended for us. Jesus promised, " 'Whoever believes in me, as the Scripture has said, *streams of living water will flow* from within him.' By this he meant the Spirit, whom those who believed in him were later to receive" (John 7:38–39, NIV, emphasis mine).

Every incredible miracle the disciples witnessed Jesus perform was done through the power of the Holy Spirit.

Think about the time when the man possessed with the evil spirit, Legion, was set free (see Mark 5). By the power of the Holy Spirit, Jesus commanded those demons to come out. Or consider the time when Jesus spoke to the raging waters to be still and they obeyed. The disciples experienced the reality of the power of the Holy Spirit working through Jesus on a daily basis.

Miracle after miracle reinforced in the hearts of the disciples their own need to be filled with the Spirit. So when Jesus told His disciples to wait for the Holy Spirit, I'm sure they had a solid understanding of why they were told to do this as they remembered Jesus' words: "You can do nothing without Me" (see John 15). The only way for them to do greater works than Jesus, as promised, was through the power of the Holy Spirit.

Whatever your interpretation of Scripture is on this point, please listen: Be filled with the Holy Spirit. The reason for this is because serving God is not like working for a company or a political party. It is not accomplished merely by using money and plans. With enough skills, drive and money, anybody can do that kind of work. But building something supernatural—that lasts for eternity—can only be done by supernatural power from the living God. So much of "Christian" work is one day going to be burned into a pinch of ash simply because it was a work of the flesh, not a work of the Spirit.

When I studied the book of Acts in college, it was all history and Greek and geography. But the book of Acts was not written so that we could study and get a degree out of it. It was written in order that we could know today, just like in biblical times, that we can be led by the Spirit of God and live this life by

His power. Just like the early Church, we are meant to experience a life in which the Holy Spirit speaks to us, leads us and guides us today and every day.

So I encourage you to come before the Lord and ask Him to fill you with His Holy Spirit. Read about A.B. Simpson, Charles Spurgeon, A.W. Tozer, Andrew Murray or any of the saints like them. Each one had their own experience of being filled with the Holy Spirit, and it was a distinct experience, separate from salvation. It's the promise He has given you. If you will but ask and yield, He will fill you with His streams of living water, and they will flow out of you to a thirsty and dying world, enabling you to live and serve in His power. But "without [Him] you can do nothing" (John 15:5).

CHAPTER SEVEN

Promise

If Jesus showed His disciples how to walk in love, in humility, in submission and in the power of the Holy Spirit through the events of life, He desires to show each of us the same lessons through the events of our lives. Think about certain situations you are dealing with right now. What can you learn from them? How do you think Christ would handle your circumstances today? If you will embrace the hand of Jesus and walk with Him through this life, He will show Himself to you, and you, in turn, will be changed by what you see in Him.

In the last chapter of Matthew, right before Jesus ascends into heaven, He leaves

His disciples with one last comment, "Lo, I am with you alway, even unto the end of the world" (Matthew 28:20, KJV). He has given that same promise to you. When we grasp hold of the reality that He is with us and calling us to learn from Him in all things, no individual is too hard to love, no situation too difficult to humble ourselves in, no person we cannot submit to and no task too great for the Holy Spirit, because we realize we are on this journey with Jesus.

I want to give you an example of laying hold of the presence of Christ from the life of Paul. Unlike the 12 disciples, Paul never walked with Jesus when He was on the earth. During Jesus' earthly ministry, Paul (then known as Saul) opposed Jesus and the other disciples. Therefore, Paul never had the precious memories and stories to reflect back on like the 12 disciples had.

In Acts 27, we find the apostle Paul taken as a prisoner of the Gospel and on his way by ship to stand before Caesar. The ship he has been aboard for many weeks, along with others, has suffered an awful storm, with winds of hurricane force. The storm has continued for days, and for fear the ship would sink, all cargo has been tossed overboard. But still, things were not looking good; the storm continued to rage on. In Acts 27:20 (NIV), it says, "When neither sun nor stars appeared for many days and the storm continued raging, we finally gave up all hope of being saved." This is when Paul stands before everyone and says,

> "Men, you should have taken my advice not to sail from Crete; then you would have spared yourselves this damage and loss. But now I urge you to keep up your courage, because not one of you will be lost; only the ship will be destroyed. Last night an angel of the God *whose I am and whom I serve* stood beside me and said, 'Do not be afraid, Paul. You must stand trial before Caesar; and God has graciously given you the lives of all who sail with you.' So keep up your courage, men, for I have faith in God that it will happen just as he told me" (Acts 27:21–25, NIV, emphasis mine).

The New King James Version says, *"the God to whom I belong and whom I serve."* And it is that statement that has such incredible strength. It's as if Paul doesn't realize what they had been experiencing for the past week, being tossed all around by this storm and things getting worse each moment. How could Paul have the nerve to stand before these men, who have given up all hope of being saved, and basically say, "Don't worry about it guys. My God told me it's gonna be alright"? This sounds ridiculous! But within that statement, "the God to whom I belong and whom I serve" we find the reason for Paul's assurance, the strength of his testimony: *his constant awareness of the unseen Christ.*

Paul's statement is powerful; it tells us where the authority and confidence behind his words come from. They speak of the basis for all of Paul's life—he had such an awareness of the unseen Christ with him, that no matter what situation he faced, he was confident the Lord was with him. That awareness changes everything. It becomes a filter through which everything that happens in life passes.

In spite of the situation and the raging storm, Paul's assurance was steadfast, immovable and confident. Paul knew he was not his own—"the God *to whom I belong.*" Therefore, what happened in his life did not matter; it was not in his hands. And it's because of this strong belief that Paul was able to so boldly proclaim what God had told him because his honor was not at stake. God said everyone would live through the storm, and Paul believed it would be "just as it was told [him]." The fact that he belonged to God and his life was given to serve God settled every issue and circumstance that confronted him.

And so it must be in our lives. Like Paul, we have never physically walked with our Savior. We don't have quite the same experience as the disciples had as they walked with Jesus and learned from watching His life. But we, like Paul, can have that same constant awareness of the presence of God in each event of life by realizing we are not our own. When we live with that mind-set, it doesn't matter what happens to us—"the God whom [you] serve and to whom [you] belong" is with you, for He said He will be "with you always, even to the end of the age."

And when you look up at Him, you see His love. In turn, you are able to love. When you see Him, you see His humility and are able to humble yourself and submit to what the Lord has chosen for your life. When you remember Him, you understand that everything He did was done in the power of the Holy Spirit. So must your life be.

Prayer

Lord, thank You for the joy we experience in being Your sons and daughters. I pray that You would lead each one of us in Your ways through this journey of life. Lord, make us more like You. Fill us with all that You are. Give us the grace to come to You, to learn from You, to walk with You and to mirror You in every situation every day of our lives. We love You, Lord, and we desire to be like You. Thank You for Your faithfulness in completing the good work You started in us. In Jesus' name, Amen.

If this booklet has been a blessing to you, I would really like to hear from you. You may write to Gospel for Asia, 1800 Golden Trail Court, Carrollton, TX 75010. Or send an email to kp@gfa.org.

Instill

. . . a passion for the lost.

Impart

. . . fresh zeal for New Testament living.

Stamp

. . . eternity on your eyes.

If you've been blessed by the insight K.P. Yohannan has shared through this booklet, you will want to read *Revolution in World Missions*, his first and most popular book.

When We Have Failed—What Next?

The best *is* yet to come. Do you find that hard to believe? If failure has clouded your vision to see God's redemptive power, this booklet is for you. God's ability to work out His best plan for your life remains. Believe it. (88 pages)

Order online at www.gfa.org

or call 1-800-WIN-ASIA

in Canada 1-888-WIN-ASIA

Booklets by K.P. Yohannan

A Life of Balance
Remember learning how to ride a bike? It was all a matter of balance. The same is true for our lives. Learn how to develop that balance, which will keep your life and ministry healthy and honoring God. (80 pages)

Dependence upon the Lord
Don't build in vain. Learn how to daily depend upon the Lord—whether in the impossible or the possible—and see your life bear lasting fruit. (48 pages)

Journey with Jesus
Take this invitation to walk the roads of life intimately with the Lord Jesus. Stand with the disciples and learn from Jesus' example of love, humility, power and surrender. (56 pages)

Learning to Pray
Whether you realize it or not, your prayers change things. Be hindered no longer as K.P. Yohannan shares how you can grow in your daily prayer life. See for yourself how God still does the impossible through prayer. (64 pages)

Living by Faith, Not by Sight
The promises of God are still true today: *"Anything is possible to him who believes!"* This balanced teaching will remind you of the power of God and encourage you to step out in childlike faith. (56 pages)

Principles in Maintaining a Godly Organization
Remember the "good old days" in your ministry? This booklet provides a biblical basis for maintaining that vibrancy and commitment that accompany any new move of God.
(48 pages)

Seeing Him
Do you often live just day-to-day, going through the routine of life? We so easily lose sight of Him who is our everything. Through this booklet, let the Lord Jesus restore your heart and eyes to see Him again. (48 pages)

Stay Encouraged
How are you doing? Discouragement can sneak in quickly and subtly, through even the smallest things. Learn how to stay encouraged in every season of life, no matter what the circumstances may be. (56 pages)

That They All May Be One
In this booklet, K.P. Yohannan opens up his heart and shares from past struggles and real-life examples on how to maintain unity with those in our lives. A must read! (56 pages)

The Beauty of Christ through Brokenness
We were made in the image of Christ that we may reflect all that He is to the hurting world around us. Rise above the things that hinder you from doing this, and see how your life can display His beauty, power and love. (72 pages)

The Lord's Work Done in the Lord's Way
Tired? Burned out? Weary? The Lord's work done in His way will never destroy you. Learn what it means to minister unto Him and keep the holy love for Him burning strong even in the midst of intense ministry. A must-read for every believer! (72 pages)

The Way of True Blessing
What does God value most? Find out in this booklet as K.P. Yohannan reveals truths from the life of Abraham, an ordinary man who became the friend of God. (56 pages)

When We Have Failed—What Next?
The best *is* yet to come. Do you find that hard to believe? If failure has clouded your vision to see God's redemptive power, this booklet is for you. God's ability to work out His best plan for your life remains. Believe it. (88 pages)

Order booklets through:
Gospel for Asia, 1800 Golden Trail Court, Carrollton, TX 75010
Toll free: 1-800-WIN-ASIA
Online: www.gfa.org